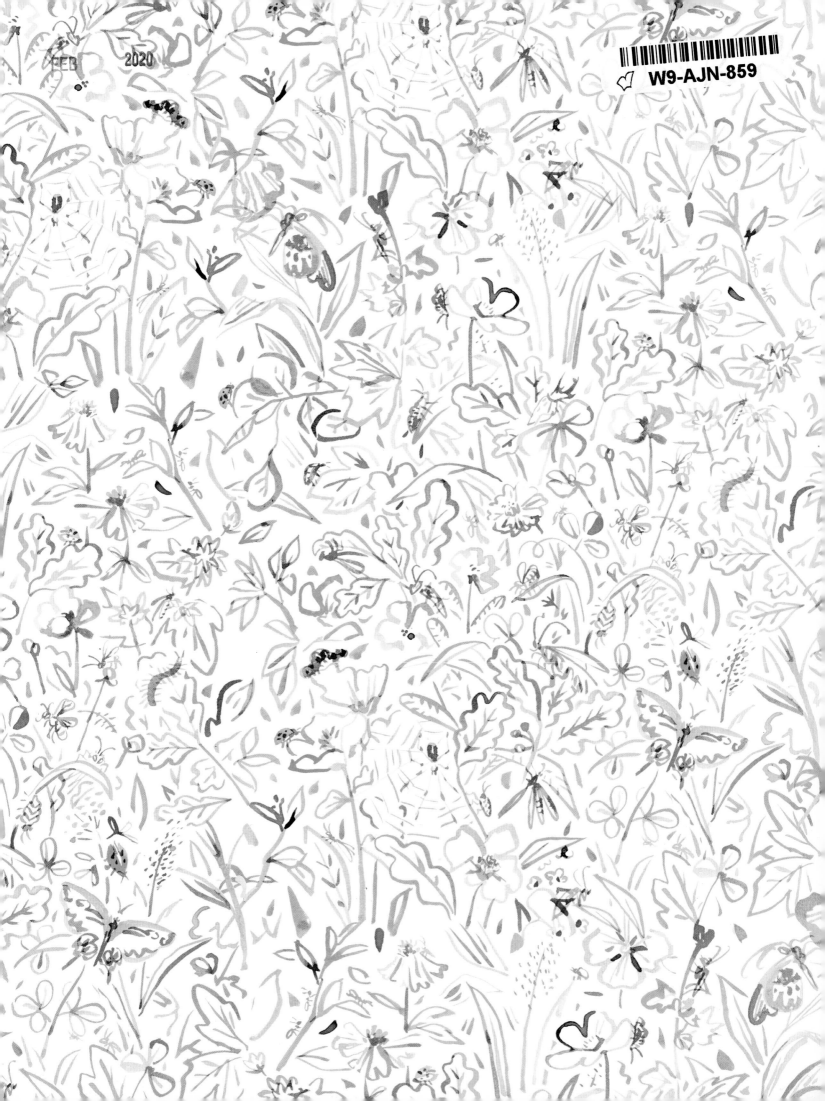

For

My mom, Nicole, for always encouraging me.

My dad, Brad, for watching over me.

My cat, Twilight, for comforting me.

Mary Lou and Martine for believing in me.

Morgan Jackson for beginning #BUGSR4GIRLS.

I love all you guys! —S.S.

With love to our two little bugs —K

Text copyright © 2020 by Sophia Spencer and Margaret McNamara

Jacket art and interior illustrations copyright © 2020 by Kerascoët

All rights reserved. Published in the United States by Schwartz & Wade Books,

an imprint of Random House Children's Books, a division of Penguin Random House LLC, New York.

Schwartz & Wade Books and the colophon are trademarks of Penguin Random House LLC.

Visit us on the Web! rhcbooks.com

Educators and librarians, for a variety of teaching tools, visit us at RHTeachersLibrarians.com

Library of Congress Cataloging-in-Publication Data

Names: Spencer, Sophia, author. | McNamara, Margaret, author.

Title: The bug girl / Sophia Spencer with Margaret McNamara.

Description: First edition. | New York: Schwartz & Wade Books, [2020] |

Audience: Age 4–8. | Audience: K to Grade 3.

Identifiers: LCCN 2019007527 | ISBN 978-0-525-64593-1 (hardcover)

ISBN 978-0-525-64594-8 (hardcover library binding) | ISBN 978-0-525-64595-5 (ebook)

Subjects: LCSH: Spencer, Sophia. | Insects—Juvenile literature.

Entomology—Biography—Juvenile literature.

Classification: LCC QL467.2 .S695 2020 | DDC 595.7—dc23

The text of this book is set in Janson.

The illustrations were rendered in ink, watercolor, and colored pencil.

Book design by Rachael Cole

MANUFACTURED IN CHINA

2 4 6 8 10 9 7 5 3 1

First Edition

The authors wish to acknowledge Dr. Morgan Jackson for his help with the bug facts in this book.

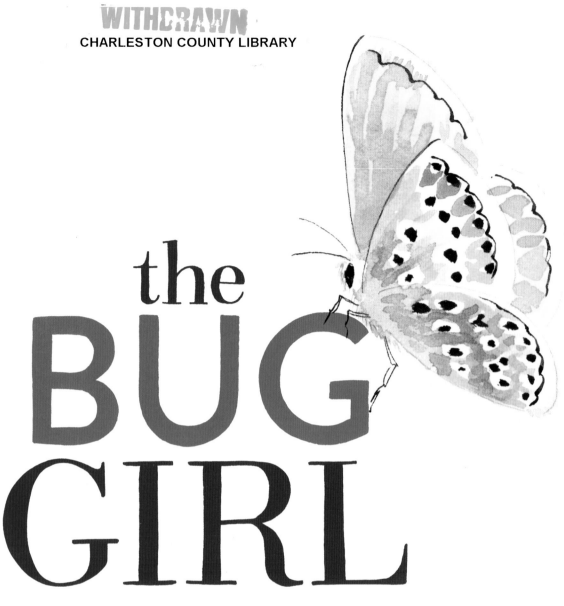

the
BUG
GIRL

(a true story)

by the Bug Girl herself,
SOPHIA SPENCER,
with MARGARET McNAMARA

illustrated by
KERASCOËT

schwartz & wade books · new york

The first time I made friends with a bug, I was two and a half years old. My mom took me to a butterfly conservatory, which is like a zoo for butterflies. As soon as we got there, a butterfly perched on my shoulder.

It flitted onto my hand and my foot, my elbow and my head, even my nose! It stayed with me the whole time we were there.

She's a butterfly magnet!

When it was time to go home,
a guard stopped us at the door.
"I'm sorry, miss. The butterfly
has to stay here," he told me.

"Say goodbye to the
butterfly," said my mom.
But it did not move.

Carefully, gently, the guard took the butterfly from
my shoulder, and after a moment, away it flew.
"Bye-bye, butterfly," I said.

From that day on, I was bug crazy.

Other kids liked storybooks. I liked bug books.

Other kids watched cat videos. I watched bug videos . . .

over and over and over.

I noticed bugs
everywhere I went.

By the time I turned five, I knew a lot about bugs.

There are *billions* of bugs on our planet.

Bugs have been on earth way longer than humans have.

They live on every continent, even Antarctica.

One way or another, most plants and animals rely on bugs to survive.

The scientific name for bugs is arthropods, but I call them bugs for short.

In kindergarten, nobody minded that I loved bugs.

Awesome!

When the other kids in my class started a karaoke club,
I started a bug hunter club. Every weekend, my friends and
I took our bug buckets and nets and magnifying glasses out
to the stream near my house.

We collected fireflies and watched them glow. We identified beetles by their two sets of hidden wings, and counted the spots on ladybugs. We watched dragonflies hover like helicopters.

We even collected stinkbugs,
which really can stink!

I took the bugs home to study them. Mostly, I had to keep them out
on the porch so they wouldn't escape and crawl around the house.

It's just Mom and me at home, so we share chores. Mom has a lot of rules:

Make Your Bed.

Pick Up Your Clothes.

Keep Your Room Neat.

NO ANTS in the House (unless they're in an ant farm).

I have just one rule:
ALL BUGS MUST LIVE.
If there's a mosquito
buzzing, I snatch it up in
a napkin and let it go.

We don't have
a flyswatter—we
have a fly net.

One night, my mom saw a water bug—
a giant flying roach!—in the middle of the
living room. She knew the Bug Rule was
important to me, so she didn't kill it. She
put a net over it and waited for me to find
it in the morning.

But when I lifted up the
net, it was gone.

When I got to first grade, everything changed. Nobody wanted to hear about bugs. Nobody thought bug facts were cool.

At first I didn't mind.

Then I brought a grasshopper to school.
I thought the kids would be so amazed by the
grasshopper that they'd want to know all about it.
But they didn't. A bunch of kids crowded around
me and made fun of me.

"Sophia's being weird again," one of them said.

"Ew! Gross!" said another. "Get rid of it!"

Then they knocked that beautiful grasshopper
off my shoulder and stomped on it till it was dead.

That night I went home and cried and cried.

"Those kids are wrong," my mom said.

"It's okay to love bugs, Sophia."

"I know," I said. "It just doesn't feel like it."

I had to go back to school, but I didn't bring a bug
with me ever again.
That didn't stop kids from making fun of me.

About halfway through first grade,
I took a break from bugs.

My mom did not like seeing me so unhappy. Not one bit. She knew I needed to find other people who loved bugs as much as I did.

She wrote an email to a group of entomologists asking for one of them to be my "bug pal." She wanted me to hear from an expert that it was not weird or strange to love bugs and insects. "Maybe somebody will write back," said my mom.

"Maybe," I said.

"Or at least call."

We thought those scientists would be too busy to respond.

But three days later, my mom got an email.

She opened it.

"It's from a bug scientist named Morgan Jackson," she said. "He wants to put my letter online so that other entomologists can read about you. Okay?"

"Okay!" I said.

Morgan Jackson posted my mom's letter. And he asked other bug scientists—all around the world—to let me know if they had any advice for a girl who loves bugs.

Two days after that . . . messages and posts
and videos poured in.

I couldn't believe how many people around the world loved bugs
as much as I did. And how many of them were grown-up women!
Some were scientists who wrote about the work they do in their
labs. Others shared videos of themselves with bugs on their arms and
sent pictures of themselves hunting bugs in the wild.

I looked at those messages day after day.

"All these people love bugs," I said to my mom.

"They do," she said.

"And they're not weird."

"Nope," said Mom. "They're curious, just like you."

Newspaper reporters read my story online, and they started calling my mom to find out more. The reporters asked to interview me, and I talked to them on the phone. My mom and I even appeared on television, which was a bit scary. It's hard to be on television when you are just an ordinary person, but I did it. I wanted to get the word out that it's okay to love bugs.

Then Morgan Jackson decided to write a scientific article about how entomologists can get young people excited about science. Morgan asked if I would like to help write the article. I said yes!

School got a lot easier after that, because I didn't feel so alone. And nowadays, I like even more things:

gymnastics,

time-travel books,

swimming,

and technology.

But not too long ago, when somebody asked me to
describe myself in three words, I said, "The Bug Girl."
That's because I'm happiest when it's just me,
a few green leaves,
some drops of water,
and a bug to keep me company.

MORE BUG FACTS

FIRST THINGS FIRST: BUG VS. ARTHROPOD

Bug is the word most people use to describe tiny crawling, flying, creeping creatures. But scientists use the word *arthropod*. An arthropod is an animal without a backbone and with a skeleton on the outside of its body. The body of an arthropod is divided into segments, and its legs are jointed, which means they can bend in several places.

There are two major types of arthropods: arachnids (spiders, for instance) and insects (bees and flies and crickets and caterpillars and . . . tons more). Arachnids are pretty cool, but insects are the arthropods I like best.

SEGMENTED BODY

JOINTED APPENDAGES

EXTERNAL SKELETON

Biggest bug: A 22-inch-long giant stick insect. But it was grown in captivity. ☹

Prettiest bug: An orchid mantis can look almost exactly like a flower. (But all bugs are pretty in my eyes.)

Most social bug: A tie between the ant and the bee! Ants and bees work together in groups to keep their communities running smoothly.

Fastest bug: The Australian tiger beetle. When it runs at top speed, its eyes can't focus and everything becomes a blur.

Favorite bug: Mine's the grasshopper—what's yours?

Arthropods make up about 80 percent of animal species on Earth. Believe me, the more you learn about them, the more you'll want to know.

Grossest bug: There are no gross bugs, LOL!

SUPER-COOL BUG FACTS

Bugs are the most diverse creatures in our world.
There are six to ten million species of bugs.

Dragonflies have inhabited the earth for over 300 million years.

Dung beetles eat poop, and it makes them super-strong.

Some **Brazilian treehoppers** have a cluster of decorative ornaments on top of their heads (and entomologists haven't figured out why).

The **assassin bug** deserves its name: it uses its hard beak to stab its prey to death. 😬

WHO STUDIES BUGS?

An entomologist! An entomologist is an insect scientist. Entomologists study insects in different environments: in labs and outdoors, where the insects live. (That means entomologists visit rain forests and deserts and tundras . . . and puddles on city streets.) Many entomologists concentrate on one species of insect or one branch of study. (Some entomologists only study insects that infest buildings!) Their work helps us understand the earth's complicated ecology and the insects that are such an important part of it.

Being an entomologist is the coolest job in the world because there is always something new to learn about insects. It's also one of the things I plan to be when I grow up.

MY TOP FOUR* BUGS, AND WHY

#1: The Grasshopper

Grasshoppers are so friendly! They are my number one favorite!

Grasshoppers live on all the continents of the world except Antarctica. They can leap a distance of more than three feet, *without* using their wings. Grasshoppers have compound eyes made of *thousands* of tiny eyes, which means they can see in all directions. And they have three special eyes that just detect light and dark. Male grasshoppers make sounds by rubbing their legs against their hard forewings. (I love grasshopper sounds!)

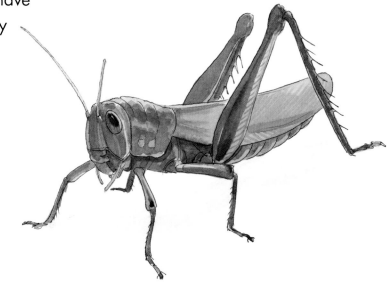

#2: The Blue Morpho Butterfly

The blue morpho butterfly lives in the tropical forests of Central and South America (and in butterfly conservatories!).

The open wings of blue morpho butterflies are so bright that they could easily attract predators. But the underside of their wings is dull brown or gray, which helps the butterflies blend into their surroundings.

All butterflies have a mind-blowing life cycle. Keep reading to find out more!

*It was really hard to choose.

#3: The Praying Mantis

Even people who don't like bugs love the praying mantis. It gets its name from the way it holds its forearms, almost as if they are clasped in prayer. And those eyes! They almost look . . . human. What's not human about a mantis is that it has only one ear—right in the middle of the underside of its body.

A praying mantis can swivel its head 180 degrees. That's backwards! And it is vicious when it comes to trapping its prey. The mantis can shoot out its arms at super-quick speed and grab its next meal. Then the sharp spines on its legs keep the prey from escaping. Some can even catch birds!

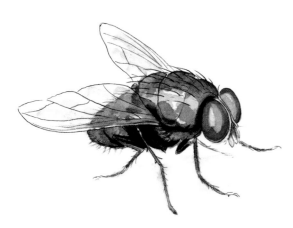

#4: The Fly

A lot of people think flies are annoying, but not me. I think they're amazing. They can walk upside down! They have pads on their feet that secrete a sugary substance that is sticky, like glue. I wish I could walk on the ceiling!

Flies live on liquid because they don't have any teeth. (They have a huge nose that sucks up food.) They eat all the time, so they poop all the time. Sometimes they even poop on their food, and sometimes they eat other animals' poop!

When flies rub their legs together they are tasting . . . with their feet!

And . . . a Little Bit About Ants

Ants ROCK!

Ants are very social. They live in organized colonies, where each type of ant has a special role. Some colonies include many *millions* of ants.

Ants work together to move and build the things they need to survive.

Ants have no ears, so they "listen" by feeling vibrations through their legs. A lot them have no eyes, either.

Some ants live to be thirty years old!

The Life Cycle of the Butterfly

There are four stages in a butterfly's life cycle: egg, larva, pupa, and adult.

Every butterfly starts life as an egg. Butterfly eggs are very tiny, but if you look carefully, you might be able to find clusters of butterfly eggs on the underside of a leaf.

When an egg hatches, a caterpillar comes out. Right away, the caterpillar begins to eat, and eat, and eat, starting with the leaf it's born on. (Mother butterflies are smart that way—they lay their eggs on a leaf that they know their baby caterpillars will love!)

After the caterpillar gets big enough and strong enough, it transforms into a pupa (which is also called a chrysalis). The pupa spins a cocoon around itself and seems to go to sleep. But, whoa—it does NOT go to sleep. It's busy building new organs and new tissue and even new limbs. And by limbs, I mean *wings*!

When the butterfly is fully transformed, it breaks out of its cocoon, wet and sticky. This whole process is called *metamorphosis*.

Within just a few hours of emerging from its cocoon, an adult butterfly can fly! It flies off to sip nectar from flowers and to look for a mate so eggs can be laid and the whole cycle can start again.

Butterflies kind of knock me out every time.

How to Study Bugs in the Wild

Bugs are all around us, so it's not hard to study them. You can turn over a rock and see what bugs are underneath it, or gently break open the bark of a rotting log to check out who lives there. You might look at areas close to water to see what bugs you discover. You can even find bugs on the sidewalk—ants don't mind walking on concrete for a while, if they have to.

My bug motto is Catch and Release! But I think it's okay to bring a bug home for a day so you can observe it closely. Get a bug house ready: Take a clean, clear jar or box, add sand or gravel at the bottom, and put a layer of dirt on top of that. Add some grass or weeds and a few stones to make the bug feel at home. Carefully put your bug in the container and put the lid on top. Make sure the top has some air holes in it—ask a grown-up to help with that.

You can look at how the bug uses its antennae, its wings, its legs, its tongue, and its eyes (sometimes that means hundreds of eyes!). You'll get a sense of how remarkable every single bug is. Before long, you'll see how unhappy your bug is in that small space. That's when it's time to let your bug go.

Final Bug Thoughts

There is way too much to learn about bugs to fit in this book, and there are new things to learn all the time. Maybe someday I'll discover something new about bugs and write another book about them.

Or maybe you will!

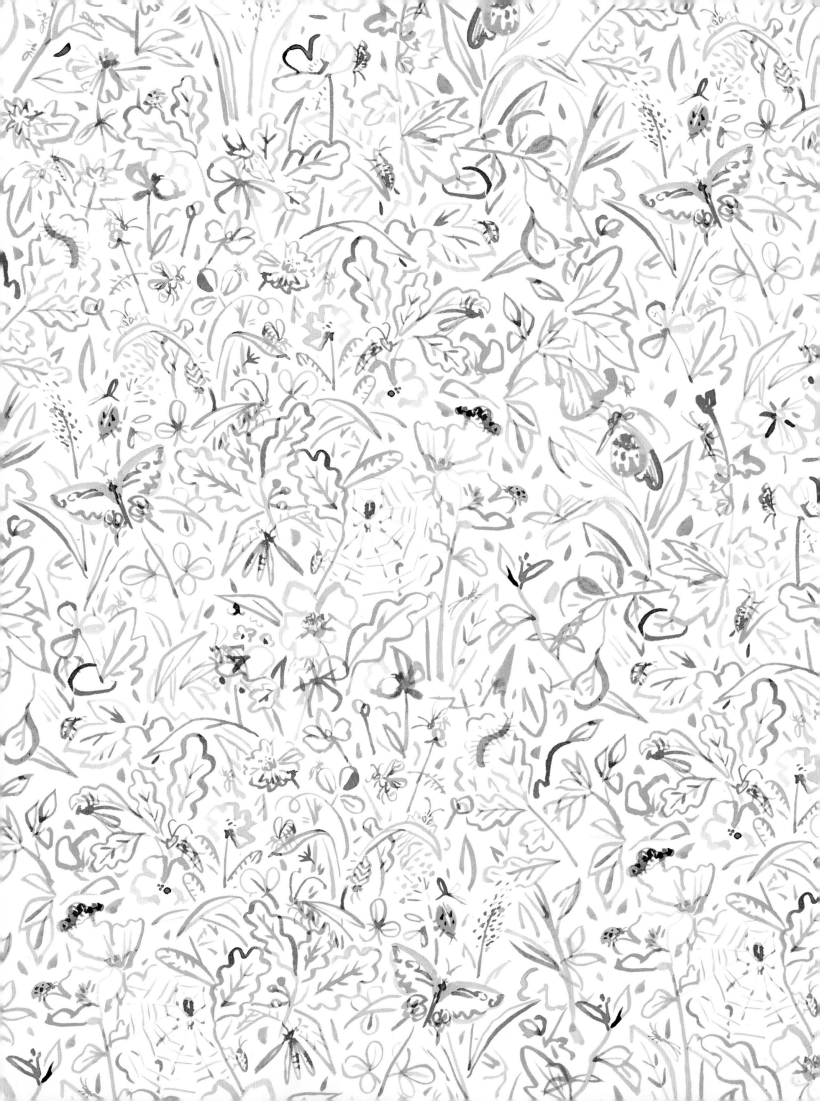